IMPERIAL
DISTRICT
WATER
POWER

IID

A century of service.

A CENTURY OF SERVICE

IMPERIAL IRRIGATION DISTRICT

THE
DONNING COMPANY
PUBLISHERS

Content provided by Imperial Irrigation District's Public Affairs Department.

333 E. Barioni Boulevard
P.O. Box 937
Imperial, CA 92251

The Donning Company Publishers
184 Business Park Drive, Suite 206
Virginia Beach, VA 23462

Steve Mull, General Manager
Barbara B. Buchanan, Office Manager
Richard A. Horwege, Senior Editor
Lori Wiley, Graphic Designer
Priscilla Odango, Imaging Artist
Tonya Hannink, Marketing Specialist
Pamela Engelhard, Marketing Advisor

Dwight Tompkins, Project Director

Library of Congress Cataloging-in-Publication Data

A century of service : Imperial Irrigation District.
p. cm.
ISBN 978-1-57864-693-7 (hbk. : alk. paper)
1. Imperial Irrigation District (Calif.)—History. 2. Water utilities—California—Imperial County—History. 3. Water-supply—Imperial Valley (Calif. and Mexico)—History. 4. Irrigation districts—California—Imperial County—History.
HD4464.I35C46 2011
333.91'30979499—dc23
2011018098

Printed in the USA at Walsworth Publishing Company

CONTENTS

Imperial Valley, circa 1912.

Flood, 1905.

PREFACE

Power to the People

At its core, the founding of the Imperial Irrigation District is a story about triumph over struggle for the public good.

It's about how generations of rugged individuals, a century ago, willingly braved the region's harsh conditions to, essentially, gamble at a chance to sustain life in the desert.

The biggest chance was none other than the attempt to tame the wild Colorado River. Successful for a time, men like George Chaffey and the California Development Company, eventually, washed up after the floods of 1905–1907 practically destroyed the valley.

Imperial Valley's life, not to mention IID's, could easily have ended there but, thankfully, the valley's pioneering forefathers held the belief that, if the independent water companies could unite and represent the people, the valley just might be saved.

The answer to that, of course, was the public's decision to form the Imperial Irrigation District, which would face many more, and seemingly larger, challenges in the years ahead.

The pages to follow attempt to preserve the fascinating and unique history of the IID, created of, by and for the people.

Government trestle. April 4, 1911.

Harvest operation with 20-mule team, 1902.

Saluting Those Who Saved the Valley

A century ago, when Imperial Valley pioneers voted to create the Imperial Irrigation District, there was no doubt what the public was voting for: ownership of water by the people and the means to control their own destiny through representative government.

The vote to put water, and the future of the valley it would secure, into the hands of the people rather than under private control, was a crucial turning point in the valley's history. After all, our pioneering families had seen the valley on the brink of despair when the California Development Company, which had tried to route Colorado River water into the Imperial Valley, financially collapsed after the early floods.

The coveted tenets of public ownership and representative government have not only protected the valley, but have also provided the critical foundation necessary for the valley to grow and prosper these past 100 years.

We proudly see these core beliefs living on today in our collective public ownership of water and—despite the passage of all these years—our continual means to control our future.

But while these virtues are central to the Imperial Valley and your IID, we wish to salute the pioneers of this great region for saving the valley from ruin and making a way for today's harvests to be bountiful and our tomorrows to be bright.

It was the courage of our pioneers who, in 1911, seemingly against all odds, took a chance that a public, all-valley irrigation district, could not only harness the Colorado River, but fairly serve, govern and deliver water to our farms, cities and homes to make life possible in this harsh, vast desert.

Much has happened since the early years. We've proudly become one of the most productive agricultural regions in the nation and the third largest public power provider in the state. Yet, despite our collective success, we remain in awe of the forethought and courage our predecessors exhibited so many years ago, and strive to honor their memory as we embark upon the next century of service.

Stella A. Mendoza, President,
IID Board of Directors, 2011

Warren Drain downstream from pipe at Station 28, October 1929.

Making cut at inlet of bypass, Cudahy Check, February 1930.

Protecting the Flow of Progress

With two core businesses and one overarching mission—to keep the lights on and the water flowing—your Imperial Irrigation District is a lot of things to a lot of people.

As intended a century ago, IID channels irrigation water to farms and municipalities across the great expanse of land that comprises its water service area. Under steady stewardship of water, people came to the desert and, eventually, generated the need for public power. Today, more than 170,000 residents call Imperial Valley home, and everyone here relies on IID to provide safe, affordable and reliable energy.

These two basic functions, both having to do with meeting our customers' essential needs, require extensive planning, teamwork and consistency. And it's a job that everyone at IID, from the board of directors to our boots-on-the-ground staffers, finds pride in being part.

Your IID is dedicated to the task, not simply because we realize that water and power services impact the lives of our customers, which they clearly do—rather, IID is prideful because we work to uphold the beliefs of Imperial Valley's pioneers who, a century ago, took it upon themselves to boldly wrest control of water for the collective good.

In doing so, IID exists to serve the public. Since 1911, the district's history has been of public good over private gain, a chronicle of local control based on the consent of the governed. Public ownership of water (and later, power), for everyone's benefit, was the intent then, as it is today.

As public agencies go, the district is a mature organization that understands its historical mission of keeping the lights on and the water flowing in the communities it serves. But while it works to uphold these founding principles, at its core, IID's business is really about protecting the flow of progress.

Today, your IID is much more than a utility. It is a catalyst for change, delivering not only essential services, but assuming leadership roles in helping to shape the economic future we all share. Our horizon has been extended to provide greater flexibility and certainty to our energy customers and water users within the district's service territory.

Similar to the hot summer day on which IID was officially formed 100 years ago, the district now stands at the vanguard of change, continuing its pursuit of the common good and reaffirming where it has been as an irrigation district and a public power provider, and what it can become tomorrow.

Kevin E. Kelley
General Manager

The mighty Colorado River. Photo by Leo Hetzel.

INTRODUCTION

How the Imperial Irrigation District Was Formed

Imperial Irrigation District was formed pursuant to the California Irrigation District Act. IID is a state agency formed and existing for governmental purposes. Its legal boundaries are all situated in the county of Imperial. IID's powers and purposes are set forth in the Irrigation District Law found in Water Code Section 20500.

June 5, 1911—A petition for formation of an irrigation district, accompanied by a bond, affidavit of publication of petition and notice of presentation of petition were presented to the Imperial County Board of Supervisors.

June 12, 1911—Imperial County Board of Supervisors orders an election be held to determine if the district should be organized under the act.

July 14, 1911—Voters approve formation of district and elect directors for each division.

July 24, 1911—Supervisors order, adjudge and declare that the territory described in the petition, all situated in the county of Imperial, state of California, "is duly organized as hereinbefore set forth as an irrigation district under the name of Imperial Irrigation District."

July 25, 1911—Order is recorded at 3 p.m. in Book 2, beginning with page 389 of the miscellaneous Imperial County Records. The official formation date for Imperial Irrigation District is, therefore, considered July 25, 1911.

New River Canal: Stockton dredgers raising levees, Westside Main Canal, January 1915.

CHAPTER 1

How the Imperial Irrigation District Saved the Imperial Valley

By the time the Imperial Irrigation District was formed by a vote of the people in 1911, the Imperial Valley was entering its second decade of existence, and the private concern responsible for bringing water to this arid region, the California Development Company, was practically out of business.

From its inception, the CDC was beset with money problems, and its principals found themselves scrambling for investors throughout the corporation's stormy history.

Men such as Charles Rockwood, C. N. Perry, and Anthony Heber pursued a domestic and international money chase for most of the 1890s, trying to secure the financial backing necessary to join the waters of the Colorado River with the Colorado Desert. Their plan was to construct a headworks on the river just below Yuma, connecting to a 54-mile-long canal that would deliver the water by force of gravity to its destination in what was variously called the "New River Country" or the "Imperial Settlement" or, finally, the "Imperial Valley."

It was not until 1900, when George Chaffey became associated with the CDC, which was already in serious distress, that work began in earnest on the canal-building project that started at Pilot Knob, extended into and out of Mexico and eventually wended its way to Cameron Lake, the settlement that would later become Calexico.

The deal he struck with Rockwood and the other officers of the corporation gave Chaffey five years in which to finish the necessary infrastructure and divert water from the Colorado River to the Imperial Valley. Within two years, though, he had completed the task, delivering the first water to the fledgling community of Imperial on June 20, 1901.

With the means to deliver water from the Colorado now in place on both sides of the border, what followed should have been a period of relative calm for the development company.

Instead, everyone involved began to file lawsuits, mainly against Chaffey, who had sought to protect his investment by consolidating his position and influence in the corporation, much to the chagrin of his partners. He would sell his interest in the company to Rockwood and the others

Old Central Main Canal Headgate replaced by Sharp's Headgate, January 1903.

in 1902 for securities that were valued at $300,000 (but when redeemed netted him less than $100,000).

Even so, Chaffey, who reportedly lost millions in the exchange, must have considered himself fortunate to have gotten out when he did. If he needed any further proof, though, it came with the flood years of 1905–1907, when the swollen Colorado River suddenly changed course, sweeping away the original headworks at Hanlon Heading and sending its entire flow not to the Gulf of Mexico, but to the Imperial Valley.

Only the intervention of the Southern Pacific Railroad, which had its own investment to protect in the valley's continued reclamation and settlement, staved off the inevitable collapse of the CDC, and with it the hopes and dreams of several thousand new settlers. The dilemma facing the railroad was whether to abandon its existing lines in the Imperial and Mexicali valleys (which were now under water) and build new ones, or to throw its considerable resources into stopping the break and saving both valleys.

Fortunately for the Imperial Valley, the railroad executives opted for the latter choice, spending $6 million during the next two years to close the break. Unfortunately for Southern Pacific, it was now the California Development Company's largest creditor, which meant its interests in the valley were secured by the continued viability of the CDC. This made SP executives nervous.

The railroad, which was also the company's largest stockholder, assumed day-to-day management of the CDC in the midst of the flood years. At first, relations between the new and old regimes were cordial, but once the break in the river had been closed for good, and Southern Pacific had a chance to audit the company's books, the railroad sued the former officers of the CDC for restitution of assets totaling $900,000.

A compromise was brokered in which Rockwood, Heber, Heffernan, and the rest gave up their shares in the doomed company, along with any outstanding water stock, and this marked the effective end of the California Development Company, whose tangled affairs were now in the hands of the courts and the Southern Pacific Railroad.

What this meant for the approximately 3,000 settlers who had come to the Imperial Valley to reclaim the desert was that the company responsible

Thompson's Crossing, the only outlet out of the valley in Tamarack District in the area between two rivers, Colorado River flood, 1905–1907.

Flood scene, 1906.

for bringing water to their burgeoning communities, and distributing it to the mutual water companies they had formed and to their own farms, was no more. The Southern Pacific Railroad had become their de facto landlord and the reluctant guarantor of their future.

But the railroad wanted out of the irrigation and land business in the Imperial Valley, hoping to cut its losses before it acquired any new ones. A group of disgruntled local investors had the same idea and called for the dissolution of the company and the sale of its remaining assets. As a result, the CDC was placed into receivership, both in the United States, where it was incorporated, and in Mexico, where most of its assets were located.

It was against this backdrop of natural and manmade disaster that the first settlers of the Imperial Valley took a series of affirmative steps they hoped would ensure the valley's future.

The first of these was the vote in 1907 designating El Centro (with its 41 registered voters) as the county seat over Imperial, the valley's oldest and most populous community (with 500 registered voters, or one-third of the total electorate).

There were five towns in the valley then: Imperial, Calexico, Brawley, Holtville, and El Centro, the first three having been developed by a syndicate of Los Angeles investors and the latter two by W. F. Holt, who underwrote much of the valley's early growth and development while shrewdly avoiding any attachment to the California Development Company.

The contest that ensued was bitterly fought and would generate lingering resentments for years to come. Holt was viciously attacked in the pro-Imperial newspapers, one of which belonged, in part, to his brother, Leroy.

But the man local historian Steve Bogdan has called the "Emperor of the Imperial Valley" personally directed every phase of the campaign waged by the El Centro loyalists, following a divide-and-conquer strategy that he admitted was his only hope. In the end, Brawley mounted its own late bid, which had the effect of handing the election to El Centro.

The Imperial Valley was now its own county and El Centro its geographic and governmental center. The first board of supervisors was elected on that same August day in 1907, as was the first district attorney, Phil Swing, and the first sheriff, Mobley Meadows.

More importantly, the valley had cut its political teeth and had the bite marks to prove it. This would be the first of many geopolitical battles to be fought in Imperial County, where politics ever since has been as tribal as it is local. Now, duly constituted as an official body by the state, it was ready to take on its most pressing concern: What to do about the water situation and, with it, the future of the Imperial Valley.

For a time, a federal solution appeared to be in the offing, with Congress responding to pressure from the Southern California delegation and appropriating $1 million in 1910 to construct new gates and levees near the site of the former break. But an unexpected surge in the river washed away eight months of work and killed one of the workers. After that, the government, like the railroad before, preferred to deal with the CDC problem from a safe distance.

But a nervous Imperial County would not wait.

Despite opposition from the mutual water companies, county officials began to circulate the idea of forming an irrigation district that would be owned by the people through the California Irrigation District Act. Phil Swing, the newly elected and politically astute county district attorney, who would later serve in Congress (where he became the motivating force behind the Boulder Canyon Project), furnished the legal analysis. He also knew a winning issue when he saw one, arguing that private ownership had been tried and failed, the federal government could not be counted on to fill the void left by the railroad and the mutual water companies could not be trusted to represent the people's best interests.

According to Swing, what the Imperial Valley needed was an irrigation system owned by the people it was meant to serve, a public agency with municipal powers similar to a city, but one that was also autonomous from county government. This call for local control had immediate appeal in an Imperial Valley still recovering from the flood years, and captured the populist mood of the voters. An election was held in July 1911, and the vote in favor of establishing an Imperial Irrigation District was 1,304 to 360.

Members of the first board of directors included: Division 1, Fritz Kloke, a farmer and banker in the Calexico area; Division 2, W. O. Hamilton, an El Centro farmer

Flood scene, 1906.

Trestle work at Colorado River Dam, 1906.

and merchant; Division 3, H. L. Peck, an Imperial farmer and merchant; Division 4, Earl C. Pound, a Brawley farmer and real estate broker; and, Division 5, Porter N. Ferguson, a Holtville farmer. At its first meeting, held July 25, 1911, Ferguson was named president of the board, and members were asked to contribute $150 toward the good of the cause, with the $750 going to help defray ongoing expenses.

Their cause was self-determination, which most people believed could only be realized through the eventual purchase of the water distribution system already in place, including the 52 miles of canals owned and operated by the Compania de Terrenos y Aguas de la Baja California, a Mexican subsidiary of the CDC. Both companies and their assets were tied up in the courts, but the IID intended to acquire these properties out of receivership. In the meantime, it would have to generate the capital needed to implement its ambitious acquisition plan.

Attorney Swing, on loan from Imperial County's district attorney's office, was authorized to defend the new irrigation district in court against several of the mutual water companies that had challenged the legality of the election, as well as the legitimacy of the IID. By 1912, with the Mexican Revolution going on just across the border in Mexicali, there was open discussion of the need for an

"All-American Canal," the first recorded reference to the massive project that would be completed, along with Hoover Dam, some 30 years later.

Within a year, the IID's headquarters would be moved to the Masonic Building in El Centro, and its board meetings began to take on a rancorous tone, as Hamilton ascended to the presidency and a farmer named Mark Rose made his first appearance before the board, arguing that lands on the East Mesa should be included in the district's boundaries.

A split developed on the board after this, with 3 to 2 votes becoming the norm, no matter how trivial the issue. At the same time, IID was negotiating directly with the railroad and with the American and Mexican receivers in an effort to purchase the assets of the CDC, which it did in 1915 for the price of $3 million. A bond issue for $3.5 million was passed later that year, and condemnation of the defunct company was initiated. Both actions were popular with the people, if not with the mutual water companies, but individual board members did not enjoy the same level of support among water users, mainly due to water shortages on the river.

Unsuccessful recall petitions were filed separately against Hamilton and his nemesis, J. Arthur McBride of Imperial, first in 1915 and again the following year. Finally, the entire board of directors resigned as a body, and the county board of supervisors had to appoint five new IID directors, naming Leroy Holt as president in 1916. It was the Hamilton-led board, however, that served during those first tumultuous years (1912–1916), which skillfully pursued the acquisition of the CDC's existing waterworks, placing it in the hands of the people.

Its reward for staying the course and acting in the common interest was public complacency and a power struggle with the mutual water companies who opposed the IID at virtually every turn until it purchased the last of the "mutuals" in 1922. It was during this period that the East Highline Canal was built, along with the Westside Main Canal and other important features of the canal network that are still in service today.

Born of necessity and tested by calamity, the IID's first four years in existence were a chronology of great accomplishments and clumsy politics, but its real achievement was in delivering to the people of the Imperial Valley some measure of certainty in the future and, with it, a reason for optimism. The flood years, and the period of receivership were behind it now, and the IID, on behalf of the people, picked up where the CDC left off.

There was only one difference, which was that the IID never let go.

Damming Colorado River, 1906.

PHILIP DAVID SWING

U.S. Congressman Phil Swing.

Much of today's Imperial Valley exists because of the vision, dedication, and hard work of early pioneers. Among the most notable is Phil Swing.

Swing is largely responsible for helping man take control of the sometimes wild Colorado River through the development of Hoover Dam, which helped lend a crucial sense of protection to the Imperial Valley from raging flood waters.

As a member of the U.S. House of Representatives, he co-authored the famous Swing-Johnson Bill that called for the creation of Boulder Dam and the All-American Canal—an 80-mile conduit that would become the backbone of Imperial Valley's water delivery system. The 1928 passage of the Boulder Canyon Project Act was also the springboard for hydroelectric power in the Coachella and Imperial valleys.

Swing was born in 1884 in San Bernardino, California, and graduated from Stanford University in 1905. After he was admitted to the state bar in 1907, he was elected to serve as the acting district attorney for newly formed Imperial County.

While as D.A., Swing furnished legal analysis for officials who were circulating the idea of forming an irrigation district that would be owned by the people. Once the Imperial Irrigation District was formed, the county allowed Swing to defend the district against several challenges. In 1916, he became IID's chief legal counsel. From 1919 to 1921, after taking time to serve in World War I, he was appointed judge of the Superior Court of Imperial County.

He then looked for a seat in Congress.

Swing's biography, written by the San Diego Historical Society, states: "As the need both for taming and harnessing the Colorado River became apparent, the people of Imperial and San Diego

Phil Swing speaking at All-American Canal celebration, Oct. 12, 1940.

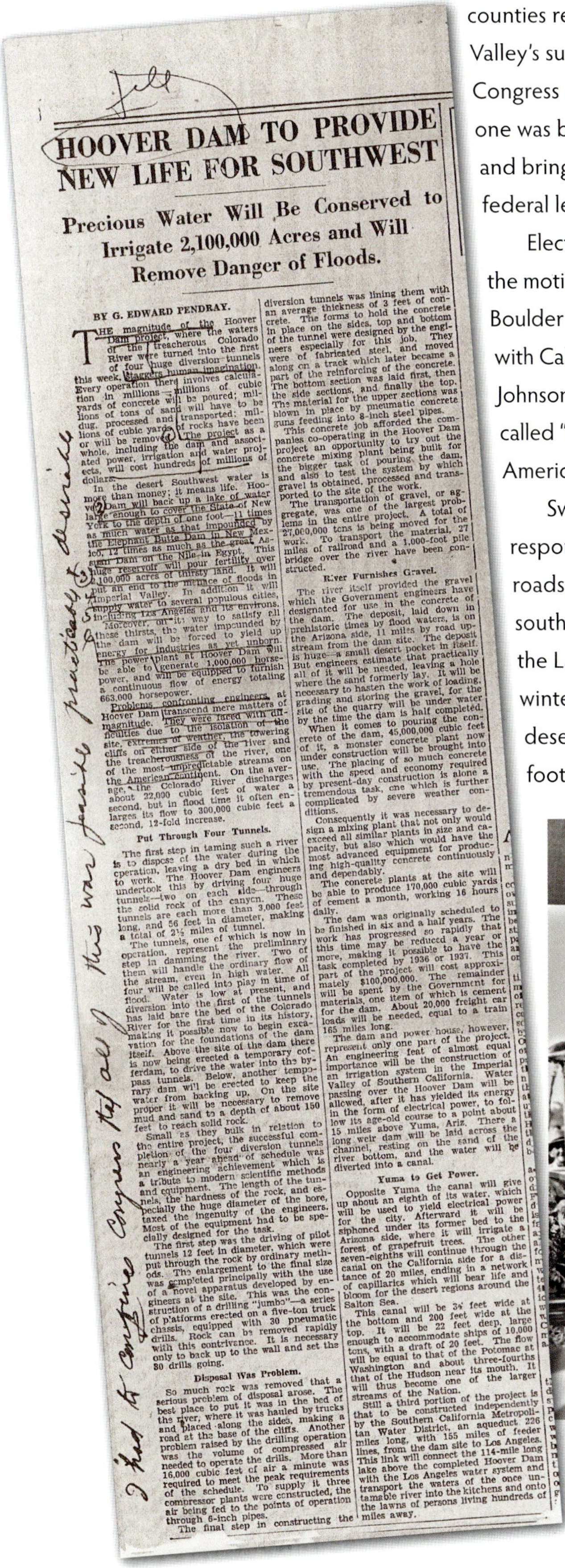

HOOVER DAM TO PROVIDE NEW LIFE FOR SOUTHWEST

Precious Water Will Be Conserved to Irrigate 2,100,000 Acres and Will Remove Danger of Floods.

BY G. EDWARD PENDRAY.

THE magnitude of the Hoover Dam project, where the waters of the treacherous Colorado River were turned into the first of four huge diversion tunnels this week, staggers human imagination. Every operation there involves calculation in millions—millions of cubic yards of concrete will be poured; millions of tons of sand will have to be dug, processed and transported; millions of cubic yards of rocks have been or will be removed. The project as a whole, including the dam and associated power, irrigation and water projects, will cost hundreds of millions of dollars.

In the desert Southwest water is more than money; it means life. Hoover Dam will back up a lake of water large enough to cover the State of New York to the depth of one foot—11 times as much water as that impounded by the Elephant Butte Dam in New Mexico, 12 times as much as the great Assuan Dam on the Nile in Egypt. This huge reservoir will pour fertility over 2,100,000 acres of thirsty land. It will put an end to the menace of floods in Imperial Valley. In addition it will supply water to several populous cities, including Los Angeles and its environs.

Moreover, on its way to satisfy all these thirsts, the water impounded by the dam will be forced to yield up energy for industries as yet unborn. The power plant at Hoover Dam will be able to generate 1,000,000 horsepower, and will be equipped to furnish a continuous flow of energy totaling 663,000 horsepower.

Problems confronting engineers at Hoover Dam transcend mere matters of magnitude. They were faced with difficulties due to the isolation of the site, extremes of weather, the towering cliffs on either side of the river and the treacherousness of the river, one of the most unpredictable streams on the American continent. On the average, the Colorado River discharges about 22,000 cubic feet of water a second, but in flood time it often enlarges its flow to 300,000 cubic feet a second, 12-fold increase.

Put Through Four Tunnels.

The first step in taming such a river is to dispose of the water during the operation, leaving a dry bed in which to work. The Hoover Dam engineers undertook this by driving four huge tunnels—two on each side—through the solid rock of the canyon. These tunnels are each more than 3,000 feet long, and 56 feet in diameter, making a total of 2½ miles of tunnel.

The tunnels, one of which is now in operation, represent the preliminary step in damming the river. Two of them will handle the ordinary flow of the stream, even in high water. All four will be called into play in time of flood. Water is low at present, and diversion into the first of the tunnels has laid bare the bed of the Colorado River for the first time in its history, making it possible now to begin excavation for the foundations of the dam itself. Above the site of the dam there is now being erected a temporary cofferdam, to drive the water into the by-pass tunnels. Below, another temporary dam will be erected to keep the water from backing up. On the site proper it will be necessary to remove mud and sand to a depth of about 150 feet to reach solid rock.

Small as they bulk in relation to the entire project, the successful completion of the four diversion tunnels nearly a year ahead of schedule was an engineering achievement which is a tribute to modern scientific methods and equipment. The length of the tunnels, the hardness of the rock, and especially the huge diameter of the bore, taxed the ingenuity of the engineers. Most of the equipment had to be specially designed for the task.

The first step was the driving of pilot tunnels 12 feet in diameter, which were put through the rock by ordinary methods. The enlargement to the final size was completed principally with the use of a novel apparatus developed by engineers at the site. This was the construction of a drilling "jumbo"—a series of platforms erected on a five-ton truck chassis, equipped with 30 pneumatic drills. Rock can be removed rapidly with this contrivance. It is necessary only to back up to the wall and set the 30 drills going.

Disposal Was Problem.

So much rock was removed that a serious problem of disposal arose. The best place to put it was in the bed of the river, where it was hauled by trucks and placed along the sides, making a road at the base of the cliffs. Another problem raised by the drilling operation was the volume of compressed air needed to operate the drills. More than 16,000 cubic feet of air a minute was required to meet the peak requirements of the schedule. To supply it three compressor plants were constructed, the air being fed to the points of operation through 6-inch pipes.

The final step in constructing the diversion tunnels was lining them with an average thickness of 3 feet of concrete. The forms to hold the concrete in place on the sides, top and bottom of the tunnel were designed by the engineers especially for this job. They were of fabricated steel, and moved along on a track which later became a part of the reinforcing of the concrete. The bottom section was laid first, then the side sections, and finally the top. The material for the upper sections was blown in place by pneumatic concrete guns feeding into 8-inch steel pipes.

This concrete job afforded the companies co-operating in the Hoover Dam project an opportunity to try out the concrete mixing plant being built for the bigger task of pouring the dam, and also to test the system by which gravel is obtained, processed and transported to the site of the work.

The transportation of gravel, or aggregate, was one of the largest problems in the entire project. A total of 27,000,000 tons is being moved for the work. To transport the material, 27 miles of railroad and a 1,000-foot pile bridge over the river have been constructed.

River Furnishes Gravel.

The river itself provided the gravel which the Government engineers have designated for use in the concrete of the dam. The deposit, laid down in prehistoric times by flood waters, is on the Arizona side, 11 miles by road upstream from the dam site. The deposit is huge—a small desert pocket in itself. But engineers estimate that practically all of it will be needed, leaving a hole where the sand formerly lay. It will be necessary to hasten the work of loading, grading and storing the gravel, for the site of the quarry will be under water by the time the dam is half completed.

When it comes to pouring the concrete of the dam, 45,000,000 cubic feet of it, a monster concrete plant now under construction will be brought into use. The placing of so much concrete with the speed and economy required by present-day construction is alone a tremendous task, one which is further complicated by severe weather conditions.

Consequently it was necessary to design a mixing plant that not only would exceed all similar plants in size and capacity, but also which would have the most advanced equipment for producing high-quality concrete continuously and dependably.

The concrete plants at the site will be able to produce 170,000 cubic yards of cement a month, working 16 hours daily.

The dam was originally scheduled to be finished in six and a half years. The work has progressed so rapidly that this time may be reduced a year or more, making it possible to have the task completed by 1936 or 1937. This part of the project will cost approximately $100,000,000. The remainder will be spent by the Government for materials, one item of which is cement for the dam. About 20,000 freight car loads will be needed, equal to a train 165 miles long.

The dam and power house, however, represent only one part of the project. An engineering feat of almost equal importance will be the construction of an irrigation system in the Imperial Valley of Southern California. Water passing over the Hoover Dam will be allowed, after it has yielded its energy in the form of electrical power, to follow its age-old course to a point about 15 miles above Yuma, Ariz. There a long weir dam will be laid across the channel, resting on the sand of the river bottom, and the water will be diverted into a canal.

Yuma to Get Power.

Opposite Yuma the canal will give up about an eighth of its water, which will be used to yield electrical power for the city. Afterward it will be siphoned under its former bed to the Arizona side, where it will irrigate a forest of grapefruit trees. The other seven-eighths will continue through the canal on the California side for a distance of 20 miles, ending in a network of capillaries which will bear life and bloom for the desert regions around the Salton Sea.

This canal will be 34 feet wide at the bottom and 200 feet wide at the top. It will be 22 feet deep, large enough to accommodate ships of 10,000 tons, with a draft of 20 feet. The flow will be equal to that of the Potomac at Washington and about three-fourths that of the Hudson near its mouth. It will thus become one of the larger streams of the Nation.

Still a third portion of the project is that to be constructed independently by the Southern California Metropolitan Water District, an aqueduct 226 miles long, with 155 miles of feeder lines, from the dam site to Los Angeles. This link will connect the 114-mile long lake above the completed Hoover Dam with the Los Angeles water system and transport the waters of the once untamable river into the kitchens and onto the lawns of persons living hundreds of miles away.

I had to convince Congress that all of this was feasible practicable & desirable

counties resolved to elect Imperial Valley's superior court judge to the Congress of the United States. No one was better equipped to sponsor and bring to pass the needed federal legislation."

Elected in 1921, Swing became the motivating force behind the Boulder Canyon Project, working with California Senator Hiram Johnson to get, what was then called "Boulder Dam," and the All-American Canal built.

Swing is said to be responsible for bringing "rivers, roads, and rainbows" to the southwest. "The pots of gold on the Las Vegas strip, Imperial's winter garden land and Arizona's desert paradise are the rich footings of permanent rainbows that Phil D. Swing shouldered into the sky," the biography states.

It took Swing, with Johnson's help, six years to get the legislation passed, which, at times, faced extreme opposition.

In the vertical margin of a tattered 1920s newspaper clipping that proclaimed "Hoover Dam to Provide New Life to Southwest," Swing penciled this handwritten note: "I had to convince Congress that all of this was feasible, practicable and desirable."

After six terms in Congress, Swing practiced law in San Diego and continued to represent IID in Colorado River matters. He served as a member of the California State Water Resources Control Board until 1958. In 1963, he passed away at the age of 79. Local schools, parks and a fountain in downtown San Diego are named in his honor.

IID Director Evan T. Hewes at All-American Canal Celebration, Oct. 12, 1940.

Clipping, unknown source, circa 1920. Phillip Swing Papers, Department of Special Collections, UCLA Charles E. Young Research Library.

Colorado River Dam, 1907.

Flood, 1907: Thousands of carloads of rock were hauled hundreds of miles to the Colorado River.

Bankers and railroadmen's party, 1904.

Flood, circa 1920, levee construction.

Old Plank Road. Photo by Leo Hetzel.

IID's first Board of Directors, from 1911 to 1912. From left to right, H. L. Peck (Imperial), Porter N. Ferguson (Holtville), Fritz Kloke (Calexico), E. C. Pound (Brawley) and W. O. Hamilton (El Centro).

First IID Board President Porter N. Ferguson, Division 5, July 25, 1911.

Downstream side of Standard Check in East High Line Canal, Dec. 21, 1928.

Looking down Alamo Canal from hill above Rockwood Gates, July 25, 1934.

CHAPTER 2

The Making of the All-American Canal

If water is the lifeblood of the Imperial Valley, fighting over water has been its blood sport.

The first decade had seen the Colorado Desert reclaimed by man, inundated by the waters of the Colorado River and abandoned by the company that had advertised it to the nation as the new "American Nile." Bedeviled by the elements and battered by the river, the valley's earliest settlers wanted what President Warren G. Harding would later call "a return to normalcy."

When the flooding ended in 1907, it was no accident that one of the first things local citizens did was go to the polls and vote for county incorporation, with El Centro as the county seat. That election, which featured a ton of scurrilous attacks and counterattacks (some of a distinctly personal nature), set the tone for all future campaigns in Imperial County, as both sides dabbled in dirt and water to make mud, leaving voters to decide which had acted the least irresponsibly.

Otis Tout, in his definitive book on the Imperial Valley, *The First Thirty Years,* attributes the pioneers' tendency to view every political contest as a struggle between good and evil, and to vote accordingly, as a manifestation "of the human desire to conquer the desert." It may also have stemmed from the uncertainty they faced in the years following the Great Flood and the slow but steady disintegration of the California Development Company.

Then, as now, few subjects were as politically charged in the desert as water, of which it was often said there was "either too much or too little, but never enough."

The Imperial Valley has been fighting for, about and over water since it first arrived in the town of Imperial a century ago. Most often, these fights have been contained within the borders of Imperial County, but there have been several times when the fighting has spilled over into adjoining areas and venues (including the rest of Southern California and the halls of Congress). In part, the Imperial Irrigation District was created to fill the vacuum left by the CDC and its belated business partner, the Southern Pacific Railroad, but it also had the practical effect of acting as a buffer to keep water users from killing each other during periods of shortage.

And no issue was more important to the early IID, or galvanized public sentiment more thoroughly, than the fight to build the All-American Canal.

In the Beginning

The decision by the CDC to convey water from the Colorado River through Mexico to the Imperial Valley was born of necessity, since it was far easier and cheaper to purchase options on Mexican lands (owned by General Andrade) and utilize the dry channel of the Alamo River than to construct an 80-mile-long canal entirely on the U.S. side of the border. It also turned out to be a big problem for the newly formed IID, especially when the Mexican Revolution occurred in 1911, and fighting in Mexicali made normal canal operations impossible. What the district needed was its own canal, a mighty waterway built of concrete and steel and dug deep into the desert, a wide ribbon of water through the shifting sands of a harsh land.

During its meeting on March 23, 1912, the IID board asked its secretary to make contact with Charles Rockwood and request any data he might have relating to a possible route for such a canal. His reply said that he knew of a route but did not have any available data on it. He offered to show it to anyone who wanted to see, though, and Director W. O. Hamilton took him up on it, traveling by horseback with

Downstream view of concrete gate and view of double 4½-foot drops, Rositas Wastegate at Rositas Dam on Alamo River near Meloland, United States.

Mexican Revolution boundary line guards, Feb. 11, 1911, showing insurgents on Mexican side and U.S. regulars on American side of the line.

Rockwood to the "potholes" area of the river in 1913. The proposed route from the Laguna Dam was, according to Rockwood, the one he had originally recommended to the CDC, but the diversion was made in Mexico to appease investors. Whether this was true or not, Rockwood, still a controversial figure in the valley, would be named the IID's chief engineer in 1914.

But there was open dissension on the board as El Centro's Hamilton, the president, and Imperial's J. A. McBride routinely clashed over issues of policy, especially those pertaining to the lands of the East Mesa. The East Mesa referred to those lands outside the IID's boundaries for water delivery, a 200,000-acre valley unto itself and a political hot potato that would ultimately lead to the undoing of the Hamilton regime.

Mark Rose was the chief agitator and spokesman for the group in 1914, when they were called the "entrymen," and began to show up at board meetings to demand "entry" into the district's irrigable lands.

In 1915, Rose's followers organized themselves into the Laguna Water Company, and managed to wrest a split vote from the IID board to include the East Mesa in the district's irrigable lands. They also approved a motion to allow private parties to construct their own parallel canal, with the IID to pay the cost of water delivery. The vote was 3 to 2, with directors W. O. Hamilton, C. W. Brockman, and J. D.

Westside Main Canal in Mexico, showing silt deposits and tule beds after cleaning levees, August 1913.

Bennett in favor, while P. N. Ferguson and J. A. McBride were opposed. At the hearing, Rockwood was asked about the advisability of allowing such a parallel canal to be built. The temperate response would have been to offer vague platitudes to both sides, but Rockwood spoke favorably of the project and said that it might even have a beneficial effect on both canals.

This was too much for McBride, who made a motion to have the position of chief engineer declared vacant, but it died for lack of a second. Even so, Rockwood's days at the IID were clearly numbered, as McBride tried twice more to fire him, only to resign along with the rest of the IID board in 1916. When the board of supervisors appointed the new IID, the district immediately hired Phil Swing as its chief legal counsel, and acting president Leroy Holt made the construction of an All-American Canal the district's primary objective. The board also rescinded the earlier vote to build a parallel canal and deliver water to the East Mesa, and when Rose's "entrymen" pressed the IID for a clarification of the matter, they were referred to the legal department.

As for Rockwood, he was relieved of his duties on Dec. 31, 1916.

IID Chief Engineer Charles Rockwood, 1914.

Phil Swing, 1916. Phillip Swing Papers, Department of Special Collections, UCLA Charles E. Young Research Library.

Early dredge "Brawley," 20-inch suction, at downstream side of Rockwood Intake Gate, May 18, 1918.

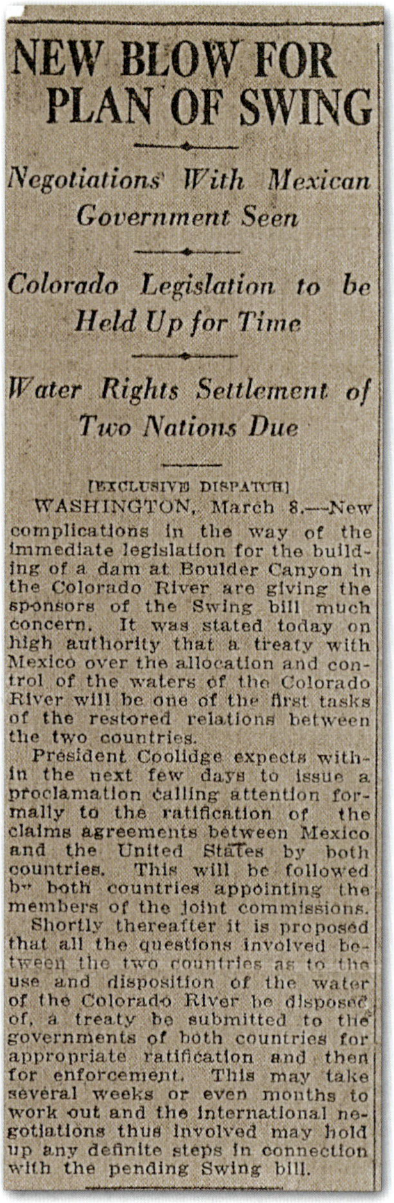

NEW BLOW FOR PLAN OF SWING

Negotiations With Mexican Government Seen

Colorado Legislation to be Held Up for Time

Water Rights Settlement of Two Nations Due

[EXCLUSIVE DISPATCH]

WASHINGTON, March 8.—New complications in the way of the immediate legislation for the building of a dam at Boulder Canyon in the Colorado River are giving the sponsors of the Swing bill much concern. It was stated today on high authority that a treaty with Mexico over the allocation and control of the waters of the Colorado River will be one of the first tasks of the restored relations between the two countries.

President Coolidge expects within the next few days to issue a proclamation calling attention formally to the ratification of the claims agreements between Mexico and the United States by both countries. This will be followed b- both countries appointing the members of the joint commissions.

Shortly thereafter it is proposed that all the questions involved between the two countries as to the use and disposition of the water of the Colorado River be disposed of, a treaty be submitted to the governments of both countries for appropriate ratification and then for enforcement. This may take several weeks or even months to work out and the international negotiations thus involved may hold up any definite steps in connection with the pending Swing bill.

Clippings from the Phillip Swing Papers, Department of Special Collections, UCLA Charles E. Young Research Library, circa 1920.

Building the Canal

Holt and his fellow appointees were re-elected in 1917, and they were more than ever convinced that the construction of a canal was both possible and realistic. Voters passed a bond for $2.5 million, and the board drafted and sent a letter to the secretary of the interior requesting "an immediate survey to determine the cost and feasibility of connecting the Imperial Valley with the Laguna Dam by construction of an All-American Canal." A communication was received from the secretary in January 1918 indicating a willingness to discuss terms, and a contract was signed in February. The All-American Canal was moving closer to reality and gained needed momentum when the Coachella Valley Water District joined a rapidly growing list of supporters that already included the state Farm Bureau and the American Legion (which had arranged a provision favoring returning World War I soldiers and

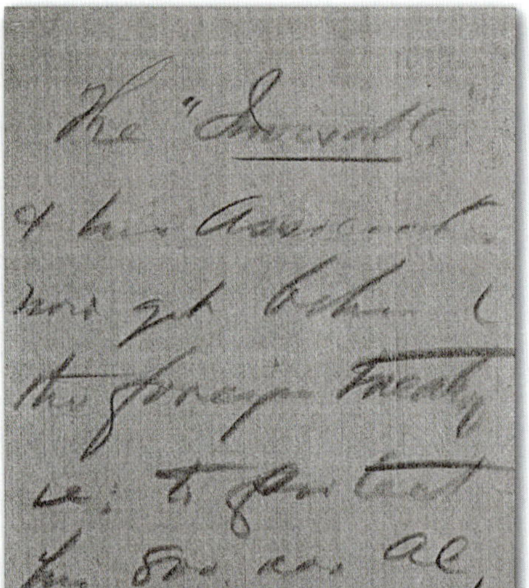

veterans in opening any new lands on the East Mesa to irrigation).

In 1919, just as Phil Swing was leaving the IID to become a Superior Court judge and voters were about to approve a second bond issue of $2.5 million, Representative William Kettner introduced legislation

CONGRESS REA[...] TO AID VALLEY AGAINST FLOOD

Leaders of Both Houses Say They Will Support Emergency Imperial Appropriation

BY KYLE D. PALMER
"Times" Staff Correspondent

WASHINGTON, Feb. 16. (Exclusive)—Sentiment in the Senate and House of Representatives is favorable to an emergency appropriation to meet the cost of strengthening and repairing the levee system protecting Imperial Valley from a disastrous overflow in the Colorado River.

This became emphatically apparent today as leaders in both houses were asked to express an opinion concerning the situation that has arisen through the failure of those advocating enactment of the Swing-Johnson bill either to obtain favorable action on their measure or to seek temporary flood control legislation.

With a flood of telegrams pouring in from the most representative organizations and individuals in Southern California appealing for emergency legislation, the only marked coolness toward present flood-control needs was confined to the advocates of the Swing-Johnson proposal, Senator Johnson feeling that this subject should originate in the House, and Congressman Swing asserting that while he expects to discuss emergency measures with House leaders he will do nothing that might be interpreted as jeopardizing enactment of his bill.

The absurdity of the contention that even immediate approval of the Swing-Johnson bill will afford needed flood protection at this time was remarked by Senator Smoot of Utah, who announced that he will actively aid legislation to meet the flood danger.

SMOOT FOR IT

"I would be glad to support an emergency flood-control appropriation to protect Imperial Valley," said Senator Smoot, who is chairman of the Senate Finance Committee and who is known throughout the nation as one of the most uncompromising foes of any appropriation, big or little, for which the utmost justification has not been shown.

"The Swing-Johnson bill has no chance to pass during the present session of Congress," said the veteran Senator, "and even if it should be approved it could not possibly afford flood protection for a period of six or seven years—or even longer."

This obvious condition did not deter some of the more fanatical advocates of the river bill from circulating a report today that the drive for emergency flood-control legislation is nothing more or less than the latest maneuver of the power trust.

Just why this feeling should exist does not appear, in view of the fact that the flood control provided for in the Swing-Johnson bill contemplates permanent protection which cannot be realized for many years, while the immediate need is for the intervening period.

MUST SAVE VALLEY

This aspect of the situation was particularly emphasized by Congressman Fredericks of Los Angeles, who has been working energetically in behalf of the bill.

"All of us have been so much interested in our efforts in behalf of the Swing-Johnson bill," he said, "we have not taken into consideration the emergency situation with which we are confronted by the serious flood peril of this year.

"We must, of course, continue our efforts in behalf of the Swing-Johnson bill," he continued, "but it will do us no good to have a Boulder Canyon dam if there should be no Imperial Valley to be served by it.

"It is my best judgment that the last-minute jam in Congress makes improbable any action on

(Continued on Page 4, Column 5)

CONGRESS READY TO AID

(Continued from First Page)

the measure during the final days of this session. The only real issue before us, therefore, this session, is that of flood control. I have not only failed to discover any opposition to emergency legislatin designed to protect Imperial Valley from flood, but have found even the most active opponents of the Swing-Johnson bill willing to support an emergency appropriation sufficient to meet the needs of this crisis.

"I would not consider that I had properly served the best interests of the people of Southern California if I failed to take into account the actual situation that confronts us. The best interests of the Swing-Johnson bill will be served and not handicapped by an emergency appropriation at this time."

Senator Johnson himself takes a gloomy view of the situation, admitting today that favorable action on the measure in the House probably would not result in approval by the Senate. He insisted, however, that probable failure this session is not due to a lack of votes, but to insufficient time in which to present the case.

LEATHERWOOD FOR IT

One of the most consistent opponents of the Swing-Johnson bill in the House, Congressman Leatherwood of Utah, who sought to eliminate in committee conference provisions in the bill relating to public ownership, and who filed a minority report objecting to enactment of the measure, said that his opposition does not extend to the subject of flood protection.

"I am in favor," said Mr. Leatherwood, "of a flood-control measure. That has been my position from the first, and I have not changed it. I am willing to support in every possible way any emergency flood-control legislation which competent engineers will recommend.

"The time is getting short and if anything is to be accomplished it must be undertaken at once."

The Utah legislator scouted the suggestion that his willingness to aid flood-c[...] is prompted by a desire to emb[...] Johnson bill's propor[...]

"I t[...]

[...]tic advocates of the bill have admitted the measure has no chance to pass this session," he asserted.

Congressman Hayden, Democrat, Arizona, Senator-elect from that State, who, with Mr. Leatherwood, has constituted the principal obstacle to favorable action on the bill by the House Irrigation and Reclamation Committee, was no less outspoken than the Utah representative.

FAVORS LEVEES

"I would unhesitatingly support," he said, "any legislation recommended by the chief engineers of the Army for an emergency appropriation to construct levees in Lower California for the protection of Imperial Valley.

"The real solution of the flood-control problem is the construction of a dam or dams properly located in the canyon of the Colorado River but until California, Arizona and Nevada reach an agreement, temporary relief through levee construction is the only practical thing that can be accomplished."

Senator Kendrick of Wyoming, a warm advocate of the Swing-Johnson bill, said that he believes "any sensible man" understands that a real flood danger exists. He asserted, however, that he has followed the lead of Senator Johnson in this matter and will continue to do so "to the last ditch."

Congressman Swing said today that he has been assured that the Rules Committee of the House will set aside sufficient time before the session ends for debate on the river legislation. He said he has not given up hope that the measure will be approved by the House, and in admitting his belated decision to present the flood emergency situation to House leaders, left an impression that he would prefer to completely ignore this issue until the slightest possibility for action on the Swing-Johnson bill shall have disappeared.

Meanwhile scores of anxious telegrams are being received by members of the Senate and the House expressing the alarm felt in Southern California as Congress nears adjournment without any apparent intention of providing either permanent or temporary relief for the flood-menaced area in Imperial Val-

Clippings from the Phillip Swing Papers, Department of Special Collections, UCLA Charles E. Young Research Library, circa 1920.

Los Angeles Times, *Feb. 16, 1927.*

Congressional committee working on the All-American Canal Project, Washington, D.C., 1922. Pictured (front row, far left) 1922 IID Board President J. S. Nickerson and (front row, seond from left) Congressman Phil Swing. Others in the photo include senators Sam C. Evans and William J. Carr as well as representatives from the cities of Los Angeles and Long Beach, the American Legion and the Farm Bureau. Phillip Swing Papers, Department of Special Collections, UCLA Charles E. Young Research Library.

in the House of Representatives. His bill, H.R. 6044, calling for a host of storage and flood-control measures on the Colorado River (including the construction of an All-American Canal), found its way to the Arid Lands Committee, where it was stalled by Representative Kinkaid, the committee chairman. Kinkaid's own bill authorized a comprehensive study of the entire region, which effectively nullified the Kettner bill.

It was at this point, 1920, that Mark Rose was appointed to the IID board by the county board of supervisors, and the pace of activity on the All-American Canal front picked up considerably. Within two years, the IID would absorb all of the old mutual water companies and Phil Swing would be on the House floor as a member of Congress, where his H.R. 11449 would be introduced in 1922. Meanwhile, A. P. Davis of the reclamation service had issued a report that recommended a dam be built at either Black Canyon or Boulder Canyon in Nevada. By now, all of Southern California supported the Swing-Johnson Bill, mainly because it had been expanded to include power generation, but also because it was beginning to look as if it might actually happen.

A Colorado River Commission had been established, with Herbert Hoover, who was then secretary of commerce in the Coolidge administration, acting as a moderator in talks between the seven river-using states and the federal government.

The Colorado River Compact was reached among all of the affected states, with the exception of Arizona. It was Arizona's continued opposition to the Boulder Canyon Project that kept any action from being taken on the Swing-Johnson Bill in 1923 and again in 1924.

Closer to home, R. D. McPherrin resigned from the IID board soon after Ira Aten became a director and was

IID Director Mark Rose was elected from Division 5 on May 11, 1920.

Ditch-digging buckeye trencher, circa 1930.

Wisteria Check, Mexico, downstream view, March 18, 1920.

Rockwood Canal gates, looking south, July 25, 1934.

named its new president. McPherrin had soured on the All-American Canal, and he objected to the constant lobbying and politicking that now consumed the IID. He made his displeasure known by joining the Colorado River Control Board, a local citizens' group formed to oppose the All-American Canal provision in the Swing-Johnson Bill.

At first, members of the CRCB pursued their agenda quietly, avoiding any direct confrontation with the IID board but, in 1925, they succeeded in convincing the county grand jury to officially take up the matter, and all of the district's five directors were indicted (including director Brockman, the lone board member sympathetic to the opposition group's cause).

The indictments were overturned when a new grand jury was impaneled the following year, and Mark Rose sponsored a campaign to defeat the judge who allowed the indictments to be handed down in the first place. But the IID board, which was now as solidly for the All-American Canal (and its enabling legislation) as it had ever been, suddenly became embroiled in a pitched battle on the homefront that would last through the balance of the 1920s and into the Depression Era.

Another former IID director, Roy Breedlove, filed a lawsuit against the IID board later that same year for illegal use of funds, in connection with various lobbying expenditures associated with the Swing-Johnson Bill. The lawsuit would eventually

Rockwood Canal: The Hind Dam as the head developed after the Rockwood Gate failed.

Phillip Swing Papers, Department of Special Collections, UCLA Charles E. Young Research Library.

be thrown out, but a Superior Court judge enjoined the IID from spending any more money on advocacy programs.

Arizona's obstinacy was the source of much frustration in the Imperial Valley, as the original compact required all seven western states to reach consensus. But the state's congressional delegation was adamant in its opposition, making the prospect of consensus impossible. Finally, a legislative remedy was devised by the bill's sponsors in which the concurrence of only six states would suffice, and Arizona was left to fend for itself in the courts (it would eventually take its case to the U.S. Supreme Court, which found against the plaintiff in 1931).

On the fourth attempt in six years, the Swing-Johnson Bill passed the House and Senate on December 21, 1928, and the longest, costliest, and most divisive political fight in the valley's history had come to an end.

Work would start nearly two years later on Boulder Dam, which, it was learned, would now be called Hoover Dam. It would take the next 12 years to complete, as would the All-American Canal, which broke ground in 1934, when the first 22 miles of the canal was begun under a "force account."

This system was meant to spread the economic benefits of the project among as many local residents as possible, which was a prime consideration during the height of the Great Depression. As many as 300 men were employed in this way, representing a total of 475,000 man-hours and at a cost of roughly $600,000.

Dredging All-American Canal in sand hills, 1936.

All-American Canal excavation east of Calexico, 1938.

All-American Canal construction.

Water Flows

The first water was turned through the All-American Canal in February 1942, and the IID would assume operation of the structure a decade later.

For those pioneers who had been around long enough to see it become a reality, the completion of the All-American Canal was the realization of a dream. It might even have been the occasion for one or more to say, "I told you so." But no one ever did, mainly because it would have been impolite to do so, but also because few would have believed them.

All-American Canal construction using Fresnos, Station 384 and 85, looking west, Nov. 2, 1935.

New River cutting back, grade recession was at a rate of a foot per minute while passing Calexico. Falls were 28 feet high. H. T. Cory Collection, UCLA Library.

CHAPTER 3

Imperial Irrigation District: A Century of Service

In the beginning, there was water.

The beginning, in this case, was 1901, which was the year that water from the Colorado River first flowed into what would become the Imperial Valley.

The river, during any or all of its periodic floods, had found its way to this alluvial valley for millennia before that. In fact, the area had long been known as the Colorado Desert, and it wasn't just because it was thought to be uninhabitable during the summer months.

No, the geographical and historical connection between this vast desert in southernmost Southern California and the Colorado River is closer, and runs considerably deeper, than the 60 or so miles that separate them on the map. It is the combined effect of geology, gravity, proximity, and timing that what we know today as the Imperial Valley, which was formed in the wake of the river's prehistoric backwash, exists at all.

But the arrival of water from the mighty Colorado on June 21, 1901, to the town site of Imperial—by means of a canal built expressly for that purpose—marked a new beginning for this harsh and arid land, and made possible its transformation into a desert heartland. This was the first time, after all, that water from the Colorado River had been conveyed in an orderly and systematic way—rather than on a rampage.

The visionaries behind its successful conveyance here were investors in a turn-of-the-century desert reclamation project and real estate development. Days after completing the long and arduous campaign to construct its canal across some of the most difficult terrain on the continent, crossing the border into a sovereign nation, Mexico, for 50 or so miles in the process, the California Development Company found itself in desperate financial straits. Besides being sued by the private syndicate's principal shareholder, Pomona developer, industrialist, and "irrigationist" George Chaffey, the CDC was so cash-starved that it was unable to properly maintain its most important financial asset—the canal itself.

And that, more than anything else, led to its undoing when, in 1905, the floods came. It wasn't the company's fast-talking sales tactics or sketchy business practices

that caused the Colorado River to overflow its banks and swamp the fledgling earthen waterway. It was, instead, the irresistible force of water that broke through the area's last remaining defense, the Rockwood Gate, spilling the river's entire contents into the Imperial Valley for the next 20 months and creating the Salton Sea.

This signaled the end of the CDC and it might have had the same impact on the career of Charles Rockwood, the company's chief engineer, corporate fundraiser and resident visionary. Whatever shortcomings Rockwood had as an officer of a commercial enterprise, and there were many, it was his vision that Chaffey and so many others bought into—only to see their best-laid plans vaporize, along with their money, in the desert heat.

Rockwood fared better when the flood was over than either the company he headed up or its investors. The California Development Company was quietly acquired by the Southern Pacific Railroad and then placed into receivership. He wasn't insulated from criticism of his allegedly faultily constructed canal heading, but he wasn't banished from the community either.

It was the railroad that finally stopped the flooding, having been enlisted in the cause by another Imperial

Building a dam across the Colorado River, 1906.

Flood, Rockwood Gate: Temporary closure of break in west bank of Colorado River from lower side, looking toward site of destroyed Rockwood Gate, 1906.

MULLET
ISLAND
240 FEET
BELOW
SEA LEVEL

Fresnos work on the Matamoros Canal, year unknown.

Salton Sea, Mullet Island: R.E.A. pole, Feb. 8, 1939.

Valley developer, W. F. Holt, and a friend of his, President Theodore Roosevelt, who promised to reimburse the railroad company by securing an appropriation from Congress. Roosevelt would leave office two years later without making good on his pledge.

George Chaffey, before he soured on the region, is said to have named it the "Imperial Settlements," but if Chaffey had dreams of an empire then W. F. Holt, founder of Holtville and so many other local cities, came nearer to realizing them.

By this time there was a significant population here, and those early "settlements" had become full-blown communities. In addition, a quarter-million acres had been reclaimed from previously raw desert land and was now under intensive cultivation. Amid all of the uncertainty and doubt, pioneers anxious to try their hand at farming continued to stream into what was already being referred to in paid advertising circulars as "the last frontier."

They came from all over the United States, and some came from farther away than that, arriving by stagecoach, train, and covered wagon. They homesteaded their ranches within established farming quadrants like McCabe or Meloland in the south end, Mulberry and Magnolia in the north, receiving water from mutual water companies they owned and, if the need arose, operated.

NOTABLE EARLY YEARS

1901

Colorado River water is first delivered to the community of Imperial, entering the United States from Mexico.

1905–1907

Rockwood Gate gives way, causing river's floodwaters to tear through the Imperial Valley, creating the Salton Sea.

Imperial Dam construction, two roller gates for All-American Canal in place, looking north, April 1937.

1907

Voters designate El Centro as county seat and elect first board of supervisors and Phil Swing as its first district attorney.

1910

Congress allocates $1 million to construct new gates and levees near site of former river break.

1911

Voters approve formation of irrigation district by a 4 to 1 margin and elect directors for each division.

Imperial Dam towers are capped and ready for scrapers, Oct. 19, 1937.

1912

With Mexican Revolution going on, open discussion begins for the need of an "All-American Canal" on the U.S. side of the border.

1913

IID authorizes a study to investigate the possibility of constructing a canal on the U.S. side of the border.

1915

Voters pass bond issue of $3.5 million to purchase the assets of the California Development Company.

1916

Phil Swing is hired as IID's chief legal counsel; IID Board President Leroy Holt (for whom the town of Holtville is named) makes the construction of an All-American Canal the district's primary objective.

1928

After four attempts in Congress, Swing-Johnson Bill passes the House and Senate, ending a long, costly, and divisive political fight in the Imperial Valley.

1934

Ground breaks on construction of the All-American Canal.

1942

Colorado River water is first turned through the new AAC.

Colorado River at Imperial Dam, circa 1937–38. Photo by Leo Hetzel.

Desilting basins at Imperial Dam, April 1938.

They also settled in towns like Calexico and Brawley, Imperial and El Centro, building churches, schools and businesses for their families and fellow citizens while trying to replace temporary public structures—like a canvas awning or crude arrow-wood ramada for shade—with substantial buildings.

The desert was blooming, and the community life that had sprung up around it was thriving, too. This would have been in the spring of 1907, some months after the flooding but not long enough that anyone had quite forgotten about it—or completely rid themselves of the nagging suspicion that it could happen again.

What they did next was remarkable, considering the environmental catastrophe they had just endured, and the bleak future they still faced. They had an election to become California's 58th and final county, voting decisively to break off from San Diego, and opting for El Centro as the county seat in a bitterly fought race with Imperial that was ultimately decided by Brawley's late entry into the contest.

In the same election, a young lawyer named Phil Swing was elected the county's first district attorney. He was also known to be extremely interested in water law and spent as much time trying to figure out how to fill the void left by the demise of the California Development Company as he did prosecuting criminals.

That election, the so-called "division race" of a century ago, would lead, in 1911, to a different sort of vote, this time to form a countywide irrigation district under the state's Irrigation District Act. But the underlying goal was the same—to garner a measure of local control (and public accountability) through the democratic process. When the people responded by voting to approve the Imperial Irrigation District's formation by a nearly 4 to 1 margin, there was no doubt what they were voting for: public ownership of water, the means to control their own destiny at the ballot box, and, yes, a greater sense of permanence.

Afterward, they reached into their pocketbooks.

For its part, the Imperial County Board of Supervisors lent its district attorney, and the aforementioned Mr. Swing, who by this time had developed some fairly far-reaching theories about how best to protect the Imperial Valley's water rights, to serve

Flood photo, year and location unknown.

as the district's first legal counsel. He would later be elected to Congress, where his main legislative priority would be to win funding for the Boulder Canyon Project Act of 1928.

From 1915 to 1922, in four separate elections, bond issues totaling $16 million were voted on and overwhelmingly approved by the public. The first was for $3.5 million to acquire the waterworks of the bankrupt California Development Company from the railroad. In 1917, an additional $2.5 million was approved by voters for the purchase of the 13 water companies that acted as contractors for the failed CDC. With this purchase, the last remaining vestige of privately held water stock passed into the public domain.

It was then that the district and the people of the Imperial Valley turned their attention to building an All-American Canal.

There is no greater symbol of the IID's dedication to the public good than the All-American Canal. From 1913, when it first authorized a feasibility study of such a waterway, until 1942, when construction ended, nothing was considered more important to the long-term prospects of the region.

In 1932, with the Depression raging and the district teetering on the brink of insolvency, local voters approved the canal project by a 5 to 1 margin. In 1933, when almost half of the district's landowners were delinquent in their assessments and the IID defaulted on its own scheduled bond payment, voters authorized funding of the canal and a bond repayment plan in the same election.

A year later, when construction began, the district obtained a concession from the

WESTINGHOUSE
BRAKE.
S.P.

"new dealers" in the Franklin Roosevelt administration so that the first jobs went to unemployed local residents. It was in this same period of drought and depression that IID entered the public power business in the Imperial and Coachella valleys, a move that closely paralleled its canal-building initiative by placing the needs of the many ahead of the few.

And ensuring its and the surrounding area's economic survival.

A lot has happened in the intervening years, but it's fair to say that if the IID didn't already exist, the people would have to invent it. That's not to suggest the district couldn't benefit from a few select changes in its operations, starting with getting back to its roots as a public organization whose fundamental mission ought to be in delivering value and service to its customers and ratepayers.

The effects of growth present certain operational challenges for the district in fulfilling its organizational mission. As a public agency, the IID's responsibility is to meet both the irrigation needs of its agricultural customers and the municipal needs of the communities in its service area.

On the energy side of the public agency, where the impacts of growth have been most sharply felt, the district must keep pace with current development trends and invest in the infrastructure necessary to plan for, and accommodate, projected growth in the future.

These are the practical considerations of growth and development, but IID must also contend with the expectations they give rise to among the public it serves. Is the district, for example, an irrigation district answerable to the farmers whose right to use water it essentially guarantees? Or is it a public power provider—the third largest in the state—that just happens to be an irrigation district, too?

The truth is, IID has come to be viewed in many different ways by several distinct groups and constituencies. And,

IID locomotive at Andrade purchased in 1918 for use in levee protection work on the Lower Colorado River, Feb. 2 1953.

as community perceptions about the role of the district have changed, the IID has been forced to reconcile these often-competing perceptions.

So dealing with the effects of growth and the change they represent for the IID is a dynamic and ongoing process. What hasn't changed—and won't—is the district's trust relationship with its customers. While it is a public agency with its own duly constituted and popularly elected board of directors, it is a public agency with a highly specific charge: to hold and manage the district's water entitlement in trust for the benefit of the public.

The IID does many other things, too, and some of them might not seem all that close to accomplishing its core mission of being an irrigation district. In fact, as the district has added new duties and responded to evolving expectations, it hasn't just created more work for itself; in a way, it is changing the culture within the district.

And that process of change is often as hard to accept internally as it must be to understand externally.

Still, because IID is changing doesn't mean that it is failing to carry out its historical mission of serving the irrigation needs of its agricultural water users. The district exists, after all, to serve the public good, and its agricultural water customers are a large and important part of that public. These twin goals of being an irrigation district and serving the general welfare are not mutually exclusive. The district can do both.

The demands of growth are such at IID that it is increasingly being asked to be all things to all people—all of the time. But the evolution that has already occurred hasn't come at the expense of IID's core business. That isn't going to change, and neither will the district's commitment to the region it serves.

LEO HETZEL, PHOTOGRAPHER, 1877–1949

Leo Hetzel

Acclaimed Imperial Valley photographer Leo Hetzel took many of the photos that appear in this centennial book illustrating Imperial Valley's early history.

Born in South Africa and raised in San Francisco, Hetzel made his way to the valley in the fall of 1913 in a quest to make a living photographing the great outdoors after he had learned, from a traveling supply man, that the Imperial Valley was one of America's last frontiers.

"His cameras have recorded the likeness of hundreds and hundreds of men, women, and children. His photographs of desert scenes are famous everywhere," wrote author Joe Livernois in his book, *Hetzel The Photographer: Impressions of the Imperial Valley.*

He was passionate about capturing images of life, as he saw it, on film.

"He was comfortable as the visual recorder of a community of characters he loved, who tamed a landscape in which he found beauty," the author writes. "In that sense, his contributions to the valley's historical awareness are profound."

Hetzel's unique images, somewhat a history of early Southern California, are said to be "probably the most accurate possible source of historical data on the Imperial Valley available."

The photographer arrived in the valley during a time of tremendous growth, when towns and inhabitants cropped up quickly. He established a photography studio in a tin building on the corner of Sixth Street and Broadway in El Centro, later moving to a two-story brick building at 126 S. Fifth Street. The studio was complete with living quarters. A skylight in the camera room allowed him to use natural light as he shot his portraits.

He'll always be remembered as a historian and the man who took all those "old pictures."

Our appreciation and gratitude is extended to his family for his contributions.

Railroad washed out by flood. Photo by Leo Hetzel.

Railroad and flood water. Photo by Leo Hetzel.

Sheep ranch. Photo by Leo Hetzel.

Bountiful harvest. Photo by Leo Hetzel.

Melons abound. Photo by Leo Hetzel.

ALAMO

McKusick Ranch 1904: south of Imperial, Mt. Signal in background. Also, McKim Ranch east of Imperial.

Boulder Canyon (Hoover) Dam site, January 1929.

Coachella Valley scene.

Hoover (Boulder) Dam: Looking upstream, March 17, 1934.

Hydro Drop 4, All-American Canal, April 5, 1941.

CHAPTER 4

Your Imperial Irrigation District of Today

Established by the people, IID exists to serve the public. As such, its twofold mission of reliably delivering water and electricity to the communities in its service area is illustrated by the public good that it does.

Because of the collective ownership of water, more than 500,000 acres of America's most productive farmland is irrigated by the Colorado River.

Agricultural water grows thousands of acres of field, garden, and permanent crops. Together, the valley's gross agriculture production value exceeds the $1 billion-mark each year. While about half of the acreage is devoted to producing hay crops, the valley is continually celebrated for producing two-thirds of the lettuce, carrots, broccoli, spinach, onions and other vegetables consumed in the United States during the winter months.

Stewardship, innovation, conservation, and expert maintenance of a reliable, yet century-old water delivery system, are the foundations upon which this agricultural, job-creating, economic engine runs.

Likewise, now 75 years in the public power business, IID's energy futures look strong, too. Having tapped into the production of hydroelectric energy via the All-American Canal in 1936, the Energy Department has since steadily, and strongly, grown to be the third largest public power provider in California.

Today, IID delivers energy to more than 145,000 electric meters in the Imperial and Coachella valleys—two distinct areas in the West that have experienced rapid growth. And the district finds itself, much like Imperial County, uniquely positioned to play a key role as renewable energy is developed in the valley. The valley's abundant sunshine, geothermal activity, wind, and biomass resources have a combined potential of generating more than 24,000 megawatts, earning Imperial Valley the title of "The Renewable Energy Capital of the World."

IID has been in step with this movement, having constructed a new natural gas energy plant to meet summer power demands, retrofitting steam generators to boost production and reduce emissions, building transmission lines to move renewable energy into the electric grid, leasing its land to develop the nation's first solar city and investigating Imperial Valley's known geothermal resource areas for energy-producing potential.

While all this is important to serving the public good, at the end of the day, what IID does best is provide reliability. Customers count on the district to deliver water when they need it and lights at the flick of a switch.

Our roots truly do run deep. Your IID was there a century ago during the valley's tenuous creation and we're here today, every step of the way . . . and for our tomorrows.

IID is fully vested in renewable energy development in the Imperial Valley and beyond.

DID YOU KNOW?

Imperial Irrigation District was organized in 1911 under the state water code.

A five-member board of directors, elected at large by the public, governs the district.

IID is the largest irrigation district in the nation in terms of water volume.

More than 97 percent of IID's water is for agricultural purposes.

The combination of water, Imperial Valley's soils, and climate allows for the production of crops 365 days a year, making the valley one of the most productive farming areas in the United States.

IID operates and maintains a world premier gravity-flow irrigation system.

IID is a key participant in the largest ag-to-urban water conservation and transfer program in the United States.

IID delivers water to more than 6,200 farm accounts.

The water system consists of more than 3,000 miles of canals and drains.

Diesel Plant in Brawley, December 1938.

Entering the public power business in 1936, today IID's Energy Department is the third largest public power utility in California.

IID is one of five energy-balancing authorities in the state.

The district owns, controls, and maintains its transmission network, which includes more than 1,400 miles of high-voltage lines.

IID delivers energy to more than 145,000 electric meters in the Imperial and Coachella valleys.

IID's electrical rates are among the lowest in California.

IID's energy service area consists of more than 6,400 square miles and includes parts of Riverside and San Diego counties.

Diesel Plant in Brawley, circa 1938–39.

IID's first power sales team, 1937: (from left) Steve Harris, Fred Mastick, Paul Post and Frank Cameron.

Above and right: Dedication of first rural power pole near Magnolia School east of Brawley, Feb. 8, 1938.

Transmission tower on Navajo Reservation, 1967.

Energy workers J. H. Hancock and Vincel Hays, June 3, 1939.

Front row, extreme right, is Lorne Richardson, general superintendent, power generation. Plant superintendent John J. Wittman is fifth from left, standing. Seventh from left is Eric P. Rittenhouse, instrument technician, while W. E. Dalton, shift supervisor, is at extreme right. In front row, extreme left, is R. A. Landry, first superintendent of the plant.

The Imperial Irrigation District receives an average of 3.1 million acre-feet of water each year from the Colorado River. Photo by Marvin Wieben.

Mount Signal, located along the United States/Mexico border, is one of Imperial Valley's most recognizable images.

IID's new natural gas turbine plant, located near Niland, California, provides much-needed power during summer peak energy periods.

IID operates and maintains the All-American Canal.

The All-American Canal, much of it now lined to conserve water, conveys the valley's lifeblood some 80 miles from Imperial Dam.

IID's energy transmission network includes more than 1,400 miles of high-voltage lines.

The IID is one of five energy-balancing authorities in California.

Water flows past Imperial Dam into a series of desilting basins before channeling into the All-American Canal.

Located about 20 miles northeast of Yuma, Ariz., the Imperial Dam is the diversion point for water flowing from the Colorado River to the All-American Canal.

Imperial Valley water delivery requires 24-hour, 7-days-a-week coordination among staff who operate and maintain more than 3,000 miles of canals and drains in the district.

IID's El Centro Generating Station, also known as the "steam plant," located in El Centro, Calif., is recently being updated to include a natural-gas fired, combined-cycle system to boost energy production, increase efficiency and reduce emissions.

Framed by clouds, blue sky and Mount Signal's shadow, this carrot field flourishes. Photo by Marvin Wieben.

Canyon sin nombre ("canyon without a name"). Photo by Marvin Wieben.

A Mexican ocotillo shrub, characterized by thorny branches and clusters of scarlet flowers, thrives in Imperial Valley's desert climate. Photo by Marvin Wieben.

Imperial County agriculture uses an average of 5.6 acre-feet of water per acre per year. Imperial Valley farmers are able to produce more than 100 commodities, feeding people around the world. Photo by Marvin Wieben.

An IID delivery canal supplies water to this field of carrots. Photo by Marvin Wieben.

Onions mature near the foot of Mount Signal. Photo by Marvin Wieben.

Board of Directors

Stella Mendoza
President, Division 4

John Pierre Menvielle
Vice President, Division 2

Matt Dessert
Division 1

James Hanks
Division 3

Anthony Sanchez
Division 5

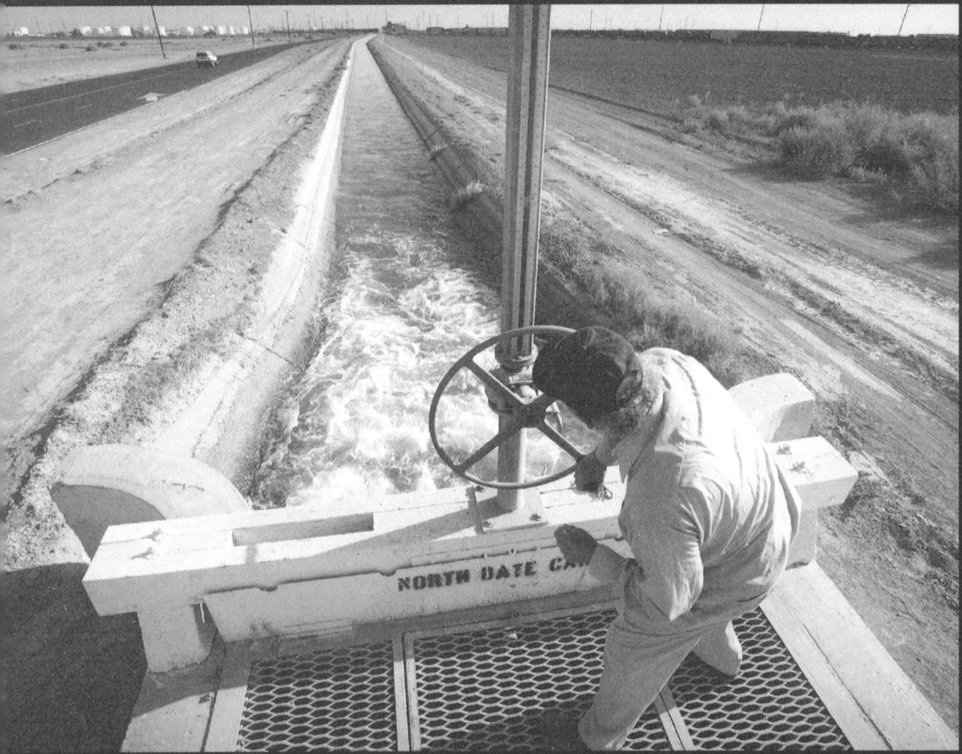
NORTH DATE